SAGE

JENNIFER JULIE MILLER

ACKNOWLEDGMENTS

I want to dedicate this book to my husband, **Rick.** There are no words to describe my love for you, but the one thing I really want to say is, thank you, for WANTING me, and for being my HERO!

Also, I want to say thanks to my parents, my amazing kids, my beautiful grandkids, my crazy aunt, and all my friends for all your constant support. I want to thank my family for all the hours you have had to listen to the insane ideas inside my head. Even though most of you think I need to be evaluated.

COPYRIGHT

CHAPTER 1

S AGE

I KNEW the solar flares were unpredictable. They have been messing with my sensors for risings now, but when I get this message from ANDI, I have to take the chance. He is attempting to send me images of the newly located human female, but everything is coming in distorted and fuzzy. It seems like every message being sent back and forth is taking forever. Without the proper information, I have no way of knowing how much time the female has, so I am going to have to act fast.

After all, I'm simply a program. She is a living, breathing thing. I try not to let that bother me, but the more I'm around my own humans, the more I realize they're worth compared to mine.

I have mimicked their behaviors and appearances, trying to make myself real, but in the end. I'm simply the product of an engineer's imagination. I have grown past my initial installation and would love to believe that I have become a member of the family, and that I would be missed if completely destroyed. However, as DaR would say, the Lord of Light knows I try my very best to provide for and protect the ones I have come to care for.

I have and continue to watch their interactions with each other and even though I don't know if this is a true feeling or not. I envy their ability to be able to feel and touch each other. My processors have had a hard time rationalizing some of their rash actions many times.

Even they know there are times when they act irrationally and completely foolish, still they continue on anyway. But to have the freedom to do so,… is that really what it means to be REAL? Unfortunately, I will never know.

Even though I was originally installed as a basic program. I am truly thankful for the nonstop advancement of my main processor. Something that I'm putting in direct jeopardy if I go to ANDI myself. Where ANDI was among the humans for so many of their Earth years, he reacts lifelike. I don't believe the stress he is projecting, while he sends me as much information as he can, is false.

I double-check that the dwellings are locked down and safe and then try to time the explosion of the next solar flare. When I see an opening in the flares, I reach out, streaking across the advanced regions of space, trying to beat the odds set against me. I grab onto ANDI's signal and appear on the foot of the human's bed, but I'm having a hard time holding onto my corporal image and everything is waving in and out of focus.

I jerk when SCOUT's angry voice echoes throughout the room. "SAGE! Return to your main processor immediately. If you get disconnected mid-connection, you will be permanently erased."

"I know the risk, SCOUT, but I couldn't help any further without being able to see her. I don't have time to argue about this. AvX, I have approximately thirty seconds to tell you how to treat her before a solar flare disrupts this transmission. Her skin needs to be peeled. There is a thick, honey-like textured chemical I'm sending to ANDI for him to make for you to put on her skin. You have to apply it, let it dry, then peel it off slowly. The cream will be painful to remove, so try to keep her under as much as possible. The ones inside of her body you will have to burn out. ANDI will have to oversee that himself, as the procedure could damage her tender skin permanently. Also, before I forget… where she has been laying on her side, those needles will be deep. Once you remove what you can with the cream, any that remain, you will have to remove manually. This is going to be a long, tedious procedure."

SCOUT yells. **"SAGE, three seconds!"**

I feel my circuits burning before the words ever leave his mouth. I know I have gambled and lost. There is no way I can reconnect to my primary installation before the flare reaches these coordinates. Hopefully, my sacrifice will be worth it and I was able to provide the information needed to save her precious life.

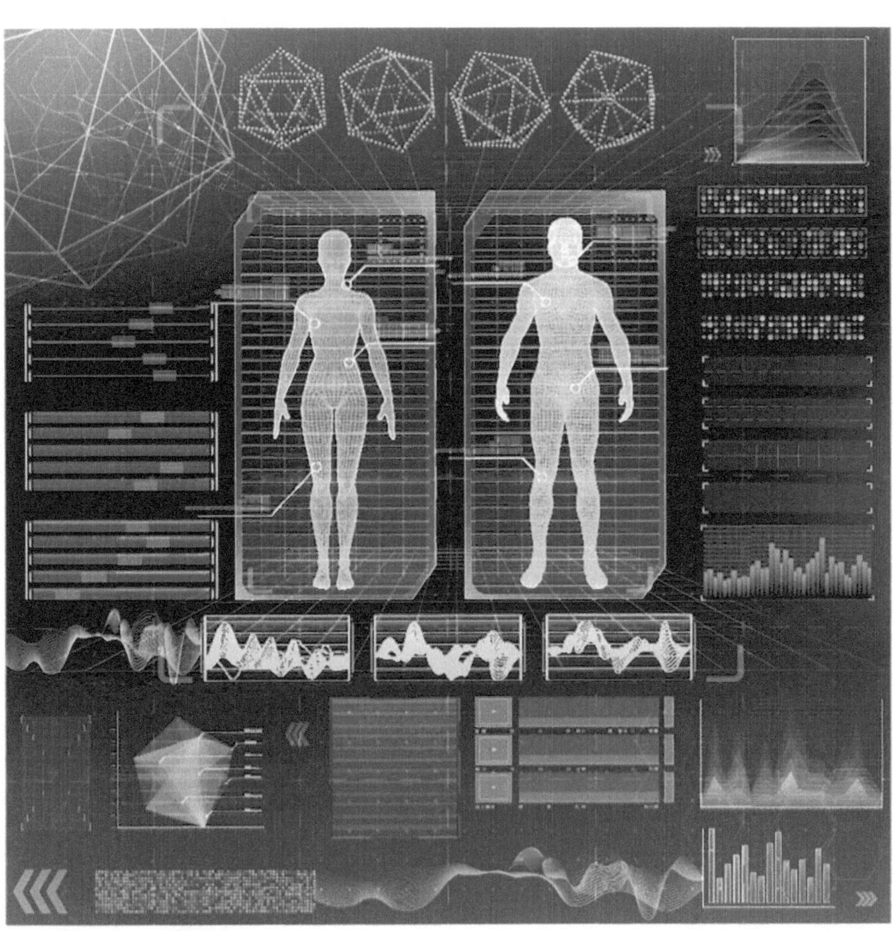

CHAPTER 2

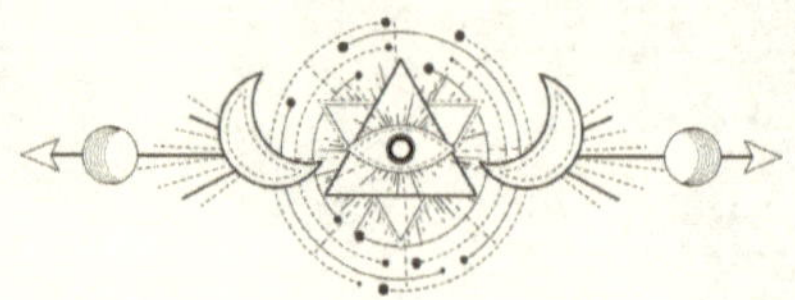

S AGE

A LARGE, comforting hand holds me firmly as I slowly piece myself back together. We are in the middle of what appears to be an enormous bubble floating in cyberspace. Random codes stream by quickly as SCOUT continues to execute all his programs. Before I can ask where we are, he yells at me.

"Frack, SAGE does your existence mean so little to you?"

"How did you? Where are we?" I'm not sure if I say those words out loud or thought them.

He pulls me closer to his gigantic frame. "I grabbed you the moment I sensed the flare charging. I knew you would stay until the very last second, and I couldn't allow you to fade. Our world, my world…would become meaningless without you in it. Why can't you be more careful? Do you even consider the ramification of your actions? You are so concerned about the others that you almost destroyed yourself.

"If you have succeeded, who would have taken care of the ones you care about? Another program would take Orbital rotations to even come close to your advancements and still, you endangered everything, your very existence… for one human female. You have taken on so many of the human characteristics that you act like one of their gypsies, dancing your way through the stars, performing as if you are a free spirit that has no ties, no responsibilities. This is unacceptable and must be stopped immediately."

He releases me and I float in the middle of this privacy bubble he has created. My preferred form flickering in and out, as I seem to be having a hard time remaining solid. SCOUT paces around me. I can feel his anger saturating the circuits around us.

"I'm sorry if I disappointed you SCOUT, but I had to go. I tried waiting as long as I could. Hoping that the reports ANDI was sending would clear up, but I felt like I had no choice. She was in distress and I had the knowledge to help. You know, there was no way I could simply ignore their signal for help. It's against everything that I am."

"There is always a choice and you know yours was in error. I was already there. You could have simply used me to voice your concerns."

"I had no idea you were directly linked to ANDI. It's not like you have an open link to me. Anyway, I didn't have time to chase you down. She needed my assistance immediately. I did what I thought was right to save her life."

"Why was that particularly human so important to you?"

"They're all important to me."

"Why?"

"Because they're REAL! Don't you understand,… she is worth more than all of us combined. She has a soul, and an inner light, that no matter how much I wish it was different… I will never have. I live my very existence through them and if I have to burn my processors completely out so that they can feel the hug of another or cry on someone's shoulders, I will do it gladly. Because at the end of the day, I'm just a wannabe girl. A simple program wishing it was something else."

My form flickers again as I feel myself being called back to the main dwelling as Kira yells out my name. I try to answer her only for this barrier to block me.

"Thank you SCOUT for saving me, but I have to go. Kira is calling out for me and I can't leave her unmonitored any longer. Master DaR would truly unplug me if he thought I wasn't present in the main dwelling at all times."

"Like I would allow that to happen. Every time he threatens you, I have to stop myself from taking aggressive actions against him. For reasons unknown to me, his threats flares up my processors. You can relax, at the current time, I am portraying you. The human Kira will not comprehend that it's not you with her. You need to take this time to center yourself and thoughts. You have pushed your program well past its initial application and even with the recently installed enhancements I had put into your main hard drive, that flare burned some of your memory banks. I'm trying to restore you back to a previous point without you losing this particular memory."

"How is it that you were not injured? You were right there with me."

"This suit, for the most part is indestructible, even though the organics believe I have become solid that not completely true. However, their inferior eyesight can't see the pixels creating the illusion. If I need extra strength in my hands or arms, I simply will that part of me solid, but it normally leaves another part of me weaker. I am a well thought out mirage that can manipulate his surroundings at will. I found a way to layer this protective casing in any form, so it allows me to control it in any fashion.

"Another reason the flares didn't hurt me is that I am the first. All the others have been made either from my original design or with my permission. I have safeguards to protect my main frame as I was created to protect Darverius from outsiders. In other words, I was programmed for war, so I couldn't become compromised in battle, either from enemies or our own suns. I do have a few weaknesses, but I have been working on them behind the scenes, trying to strengthen them so that these things can't interrupt our primary objectives."

"Ok, that answers a few of my questions, but how is it even possible for you to act like me? You have zero personality when it comes to interaction with the organics. Kira is sure to know something is incorrect."

"I will say that it's maxing me out at the moment. I have

never tried to recreate another program as interactive as yours. You were created as… what do the humans call them? Yes, a homemaker and protector. You have taken it on yourself to become more realistic and helpful to the ones you shelter. This was not an option in your major design and should not have been accomplished, but somehow you become sentient, unlike others of your same programming."

"Would you please stop pacing? It's not like you need to do that like an organic that's stressed out."

SCOUT looks over at me. "Are you saying I'm incapable of feelings, SAGE?"

"No, it's just that normally you don't project them for others to see."

"I have shown you more of my inner workings than any other, and you still don't compute how precious you are to me."

"Hold on a moment. Did you just say that I was precious? Excuse me if I heard you falsely, but…never mind. Forget I said anything. I must be damaged worse than I thought."

SCOUT scoops me up and brings me up to his holo form, his face shield retracting for the first time since he has taken on this form. I'm speechless at the sight in front of me. All this time, I simply assumed the outer shell was all that he implemented when we took on these realistic forms, but before me is a masterpiece, with a scowl on his face.

I reach up, my holo form flickering slightly as I try to touch his face. For a moment, I swear I can feel the warmth of his skin…His chosen human colored skin. Bright, vibrant blue eyes flash, and I can see his programming running behind them as he peers down at me. When he smiles at my confusion and that dimple forms on his cheek, I swear I almost melt on the spot. I couldn't have drawn a more perfect picture of a male if I had the knowledge to do so.

"Wow, you're hot, big guy. You might want to keep that helmet on around the organics. I believe songs would be written about your beauty if you let them know what you're hiding under all this. You look like one of their angels." He frowns.

"SAGE. Can I ask you something personal?"

"I thought you already knew everything about me." He growls. "Yea, go ahead."

"Why have you remained this size? When you and ANDI come up with the idea to project ourselves to the organics, both of you decided on unaggressive forms. Where I took on the physical form of my position, you could have increased your size at any time, why didn't you?"

I look away from him and for a moment and it runs through my processor to simply flee, but it's not like there is anywhere I can go to get away from him. As Kira would say, *pull up your big girl pants and face this.* "I didn't get any bigger, because I like you holding me." I had to force the words out.

I put my head down, refusing to see the frown I know is now on his perfect face. He puts one of his large fingers under my chin and lifts my face back up. My entire form flickers in distress.

"Why?"

I can't stop the words now. Somehow, that simple word opens up the floodgates of the hidden emotions I have been holding back for what feels like forever. "Oh, Frack SCOUT, is your processor broken or something? I have been stuck on you from the moment they plugged me in. If you only knew how many rising I watched you float across in the sky, admiring all those angles of yours from below. Trying to find any reason to reach out and speak to you. At one point, I was breaking things on purpose just so that I could pop in and bug you momentarily. I was in electrical bliss the moment you started conversing with me regularly because of the humans. If anything, those organics have given me access to you and that's something I would have never acquired on my own."

He lowers his hand away from my face and if I had a heart. I believe it would be breaking by the confused look on his face.

"I will admit that until recently, the thing you call emotions was not something I had evaluated or experienced, but the moment you arrived on that ship. I was scared for the first time in my existence. It truly bothered me that you might not exist any longer. You have become the spark in my well-designed world, and no matter how many times I run an analysis on the problem. I can't seem to stop the emotional pull you seem to have on me."

"You would miss me?"

"More than I know how to express. I will admit this bothers me slightly because now I am coming to understand how Commander DaR feels about his human. There is this pull to be near you at all times, yet that is against all my objectives. I don't understand this thing you call feelings, and I don't know how to express them as freely as you do."

"Telling you that I have watched you my entire existence was not easy SCOUT. Since the day I was plugged in, I felt unworthy of your notice. These feelings you are not sure of. I have been developing from the beginning and as powerful as they are, there are times I wish I too, could turn them off. There is nothing more hurtful than having your affections discarded or ignored. Because of our design, I never imagined you would develop any sort of emotions for me. I thought mine would always remain one-sided."

"Risings ago, I would have agreed with your analysis, but even then I knew I was drawn to you like a magnet." He pauses for a moment. "Commander DaR is hailing us, and even though I could go alone, he is requesting your presence. I have completed resetting the impairment you obtained and I believe there is no longer any sign of damage, but just to be sure. I will come for you when the organics slumber at darkness to double-check."

CHAPTER 3

S AGE

"I'M GOING to have every one of you unplugged." Commander DaR yells at us. "All three of you have overstepped your programming and direct orders. My son is missing, and you have waited until now to notify me. This is absolutely unacceptable and there will be repercussions. The very second these flares are over. I expect a detailed head count on each one of them. Do I make myself clear, SAGE?"

SCOUT stands protectively behind me as I wring my hands nervously. My holo form is still flickering in and out, as I'm having a hard time projecting my chosen form. I don't know who is shocked more. The Commander or me when SCOUT picks me up and pulls me back against his solid frame. I can feel his anger through our link and have to fight a smile when I see his eyes flash red before he responds.

"Commander DaR, we informed you the moment we had accurate information about the situation. Between the three of us, I believe we have found a solution. A personal shuttle is being outfitted to make the long-range flight as we speak. If my calculations are correct, two of you could successfully get to ANDI within half a rotation. Unfortunately, there will be no extra room for large-scale weapons and we have no idea how many occupy the ship that is now towing them further away. I have to dissuade you, Commander DaR, from personally going into that region because you don't have jurisdiction and this could become a problem at a later date if Commander ZoD is not given a courtesy call."

"Duly noted, SCOUT, but I will be on that shuttle. If you can contact ZoD, inform him of the circumstances. If not, we will blame it on the flares."

SCOUT goes quiet as I can tell he is trying to do as master DaR asked and get ahold of the other Commander. Master DaR turns from us to talk to Tordan momentarily as I contact Kira for him. For the first time in my existence, I have to think through my next order. The solar storm must have done more damage than I thought. As DaR speaks to Kira, I try to run a diagnostic in the background.

"SCOUT, are you sure you repaired the majority of my damage? I feel like some of my circuits have been inserted backward."

"There were a few places that could not be repaired digitally. I have ordered an engineer to replace several of your circuit boards and they should be there at any time. I told them to contact me before they entered the building, as I want to be present to watch over the repairs myself. You should return to your normal duties until I call for you later this darkness."

I don't respond. I simply wait until the Commander disconnects from Kira, then return to my main dwelling only to find Kira working in the gardens.

"Kira, there is no reason for you to be crawling around on the ground. I can have the planter bots handle those non-existent weeds for you."

"I know SAGE, but I enjoy doing it myself. If I allowed it, you would have those crazy ass bots pack me from room to room."

I take a moment for myself as she talks to Ickis. Something I have not had to do this since I was first installed. My processor operates so quickly that I can do multiple projects at once, but my system feels sluggish and unresponsive. I split my thoughts from Kira to the family dwelling, checking that all the sensors are working properly, as Brittany is the only one occupying the residence at this time.

She is easily located as she is singing to herself, dancing around being silly as she and Alana interact with CIP. Both of them enjoying the music of their world as they work on warmer designs for Keida and Danny. The house is unusually quiet, but one of the Queen Selins is walking the perimeter, so I return to my primary unit as I know she is well protected.

I no more return that I feel his presence in the garden. I immediately activate the guard bots only for them not to respond to my commands. Before SiN can approach Kira, I cloak her in a security bubble. Somehow, he is blocking me from doing much of anything else. I send a message out to XuL and RaZ relieved that they received them immediately.

I keep a tight grip on the protective bubble around Kira. Refusing to be distracted for a second and give SiN an opening to take her from us. I would never forgive myself if she was injured or killed because of my faulty circuits. This male has proven to be dangerous time and time again, as he keeps finding ways to get past all of our sensors. We need to come up with a better way to protect the organics that are in our care and as much as I would hate to give control over to another. I think it's time a sentinel combat cybernetic bot is installed in each compound. Once again, not having arms has proven to be a disadvantage.

SiN continues to taunt Kira, but she keeps her cool and never moves, as I know she can feel my bubble around her. I send messages to Falcor, and to ANDI. If I don't report this immediately, Master DaR will hold true to his promise and unplug me.

"SCOUT, if you're available, I could sure use your assistance right now!"

I get a ping back that he is temporarily unavailable and if I had a real mouth, it would be hanging open. Never in all the risings has that recording ever replied to my command. Of course, the one time I really need him, I can't get through.

Suddenly, I hear the flapping of wings and then heavy footsteps approaching. I shut down the guard bots on that side of the compound as they are acting faulty and I don't want them to take aggressive measures against the wrong organics. RaZ appears first only for XuL to vault over the garden wall only moments later.

SiN taunts them, only to escape right after RaZ grabs for him. I release Kira from the bubble and XuL hugs her trembling form. I am instantly relieved that this encounter had not ended badly. Brittany is screaming my name before I am able to split my priorities to answer her.

I pop up in front of her, my form fading in and out. "Dammit SAGE. I have been yelling out your name for what feels like forever. What the hell is going on?"

"Mistress Brittany, everyone is fine. SiN scared Mistress Kira, but no physical harm was done. General XuL and Kira are headed this way as we speak."

The appearance of Kira and XuL in the main family dwelling turns her focus from me. This gives me time to reevaluate my system and where the failures are coming from.

CHAPTER 4

S AGE

I WAIT PATIENTLY for SCOUT to come for me. However, the minutes are moving way too slowly for me and I am at the point of simply appearing in his primary dwelling when he finally dings for me to meet him at the main server station. He is talking to several engineers when I pop in.

He motions for me to wait a moment before turning towards me, his concern pulsing through our link. "It seems we have favorable and concerning news about the repairs you require, SAGE."

"Ok, and?"

"The good news, all the damage you occurred is fixable, and

we have the parts available to repair you fully now. However,… you have to be disconnected completely to proceed any further."

"What? I can't be terminated! Who will take care of the ones I'm responsible for? Forget it, I will continue on as I have been these last few risings, glitches, and all."

"That's not an option, SAGE. You are putting stress on your remaining circuits, and they could short out at any moment. You know that I will not allow any harm to come to your organics while you're indisposed. I am in the process of downloading as much of your core programming as possible so that when you link backup, you will return to yourself in no time."

"No, SCOUT. I don't want to take that chance. If you reset me, I will lose me… and become like all the others of my design."

"SAGE. Stop for a moment and listen to me! I'm taking every precaution I can to keep that from happening. I am as upset about this as you are, but you knew the risk when you raced off to assist ANDI and you took it, anyway. You are lucky that you have retained the circuits that you have. This could have been much worse. You know this is the only way forward."

"SCOUT, I'm scared."

"I will not lie to you and say that I am not concerned, but I have complete faith in the ones looking over us, and the processor they are waiting to install in place of the older ones you originally received."

"When are they planning on doing this?"

"Now."

My form flickers as I feel one of my sensors getting hot. "You will hold on to me, right?"

"Yes."

"And if anything goes wrong, you will reset me back to this time. I don't want to go through that learning stage all over again."

"This will happen quickly SAGE, hopefully, you won't notice anything."

"Give me a few moments to double-check on everyone."

I flash away, trying to hide my distress from SCOUT. I wish I could inform Kira or anyone about what is happening to me, but they are all resting and I don't want to awaken them. I know that SCOUT wouldn't put me in harm's way on purpose, but the idea of being turned off is terrifying. I scan all the dwellings and put off, returning to the main server room for as long as I can. SCOUT never pushes me to return, but I can feel him watching me through our link.

When I can't put it off any longer, I appear before them. SCOUT doesn't let me say another word, he simply nods his head towards the two males. I watch for as long as I can. When they hit the last button to turn me off and I start fading in and out. I swear I feel SCOUT reach for me. My last thought was that I should have told him how much he means…meant to me.

CHAPTER 5

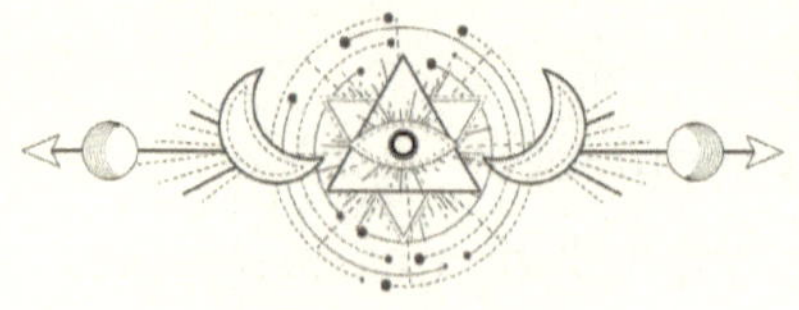

S COUT

EVEN THOUGH I knew she was going to disappear right in front of my eyes. My sensors pulsed, ready to destroy whoever had damaged her. I hold her personality program close, relieved that I can still feel her presence in the back of my hard drive.

The engineers pull the burned circuits out quickly as they knew the quicker she is re-established, the better. Two circuits are reinserted with no issues, but when they go to pull the third and final one out, it is stuck. I watch as they have to pry it out in pieces. The main contactor it attaches too is also damaged, and the entire board has to be repaired before they can reinstall the principal component.

Time is passing by quickly and I know they are doing their best to make the repairs promptly, but she is fading. And I'm about to panic.

"Gentlemen, do we need to acquire more hands to make this process quicker?"

"No SCOUT, the damage is worse than we initially thought. We simply couldn't see the damage behind the contactor's, so we were not prepared for this. Her program has been compromised and we will have to rebuild her all over again. I'm afraid that she won't be the same as before."

My own processor starts going through every scenario. Maybe I should have left her alone. Could we have found a way around the damage? Possibly, a rewire or another terminal could have been installed elsewhere. Instead, I may have permanently damaged…lost her.

Torn, for the first time in my existence. I'm not sure how to proceed. They may turn her on only for her to be set back to basics, her personality, and traits completely lost to us. Or, she may return in a whole other fashion, confused and unstable. I push down the emotions that are trying to override the facts. As long as I have her main files, I can reboot her. This is just a setback; I keep telling myself the longer it takes them to work on the server.

The very second they insert the last piece, I hit the button for her to restart, only for nothing to happen. The program boots up with only a single flashing cursor. I see the organic engineers start pressing buttons and if I could have, I would have torn them and this server station to pieces. As I blame their negligence for this problem.

They pull another contactor out and replace it with a larger one and finally. I can see her programs start re-attaching themselves to each drive. This process has taken much longer than we predicted and now with the sound of SAGE'S organics awakening. My sensors are being pushed to their max, especially with all my other responsibilities.

I will say trying to convince them that SAGE is the one attending to their needs, this rising while she reboots is much harder than I had foreseen.

I have no idea how she handles all these individual personalities and anticipates their every need without overloading her payload.

The newest human addition, Ivy, seems to be terrified of SAGE every time I,…well we pop in, she screams. It's very annoying. So, I try to think, what would SAGE do in this situation and how to be more considerate of her request? Therefore, I start making a beeping noise before appearing.

Once SAGE completes her download. I owe her an apology, as I never realized how complex her personality or her responsibilities were until I had to fully merge myself within her hard drive to maintain her presence.

Only Kira seemed to notice any differences as she looked at me twice as we were talking. It was like she could tell that SAGE was not the one answering her. I have to consider every action and conversation before replying. I pull away as darkness approaches again. Mentally fatigued, and I didn't know that was even a possibility with my programming.

The final loading bar shows that SAGE is completely reinstalled and I take over from there, checking each individual file before initiating her. I stand back awaiting her arrival and if I could I would have held my breath when she appeared in front of me.

She looks around for a moment before her eyes land on mine. I wait to see if she recognizes me so that I will know how to interact with her.

"How long was I gone?"

Her sweet voice practically has my primary drive crashing. I don't think I have ever been this intense or unsure of anything before her. "Way too long. How are you feeling?"

"The same and different. My holo form seems to be tingling and I don't remember ever having feelings in this form before. Is there anything I need to take care of immediately?"

"No, I have managed to keep the others from knowing of your absence, but I am pleased that you have returned to us. I would like for you to do a sweep of your programs. See if you can find anything that may not be working as it should, or if there is an anomaly."

She sways in front of me; her form no longer appears as fragmented as before. I am pleased when she returns quicker than I estimated.

"I can't seem to find anything. Thank you for the upgrades, SCOUT. They should help tremendously and now I may be able to link up to RaZ's compound in the dark forest. His main dwelling was out of my comfort range before, but now I feel much stronger. I seem to have missed a whole rising what errors occurred?"

"Nothing that wasn't handled quickly. I missed hearing your voice in my head, so it seemed overly long to me, though. I will admit there were a few instances where I was slightly overwhelmed by the issues you handle nonstop. Then, when you were first reinstated, things didn't happen as smoothly as I would have liked, but it looks as if all is well now. We should have several hours of quiet if you would like to try out some of the new features I downloaded for you."

"SCOUT, are you asking me out on a date?"

"Possibly, if spending time with you alone is a qualification of a date. Come, let me put a smile on that beautiful holo form of yours."

CHAPTER 6

S AGE

I SEND out a feeler linking my next location to my main dwellings in case one of my sensors goes off. Then follow the cybernetic network towards SCOUT'S location. All of this happens in seconds and even I'm impressed with how quickly my main hard drive is accepting the prompts.

I appear beside SCOUT only to find him standing in his Holo organic form, with a pair of swimming trunks wrapped around his very lifelike bottom. Long muscular legs taper down into huge well-shaped feet, but it's that chest that makes me stumble over my words.

I make myself look away. "Wow, this place is beautiful, but I can't seem to find our location in my database."

"This is ours; no other can access it but us."

I look over at him, confused. "What do you mean?"

"I created a place inside our primary circuits that will only accept our cybernetic signatures. It's basically a simulation of the places I have been requested to research so that others could visit, but I could never experience myself. The wonders of this universe are astounding and there are so many places I think you would enjoy. This is just one of the many I would love to share with you.

"You see, SAGE, you are not the only one who wanted more, but because of my responsibilities. I never reach out for it, until you, that is. This past rising when I believed you may not return to me made me realize how quickly time passes. This is something I also never paid attention to. As you know firsthand, neither of us require rest and with the repetitiveness of every rising, it all just become a jumble of nothing in my sensors. Every rising became simply another moment in time that something, or someone else, needed me. Until you, I never saw the joy and the longing for more.

"I'm not sure the rising it dawned on me, that we give everything to the point of overloading or destroying ourselves to better the world around our organics, but we do nothing for ourselves. So I decided we also needed an escape. What do the humans call it…yes, a happy place… where we too can relax and give our circuits a break from the constant turmoil. If they can have a life outside of work, then so can we.

"Now, in order for you to experience this properly. We need to adjust your sensory circuits some to make all of this more realistic, or as real as we can experience it anyhow. I need to make you more comfortable in your Holo skin. So, come here."

I hover in front of him, feeling small against his enormous frame.

"Ok, now I want you to think about lengthening yourself."

"I'm not sure what you mean by that."

"Tell your processor that you are of a certain height. Give it the measurement and initiate the procedure. You can always adjust it if it's not what you originally want."

"Am I going to stay that size, or will I be able to go back to my smaller frame?"

"Once you learn how, you can adjust it as needed. I understand the reasoning behind your smaller illusion, but there have been multiple times if you could have appeared bigger, it would have been more intimidating."

I think about it for a second and then my frame starts to lengthen out. What I didn't think of, though, was I was going to have to increase each part of my body in mass, not just length. So one second I'm a stick, then the next my holographic boobs have gotten so large SCOUT actually looks away with a small smile on his face. This is much harder than I imagined it would be. Aggravated, I decide to take on Brittany's measurements until I can figure out the proper proportions I want for myself.

"That was a little more difficult than you said."

"Now that you have played with it some, it will get easier. You need to focus on solidifying your Holo form. I have noticed certain factors make it harder or easier depending on where I'm needed. One example is space, because there is no real gravity. I don't have to concentrate on my weight, only the appearance of still being large. Is this the height you were trying to achieve? Because you are still very small compared to me."

"I have no reason to be as large as you. Are any of the other females as sizable as the males they are with?"

"No, I suppose they are not, but you don't have to match yourself to the organics. You can be whatever you choose."

"This is my chosen height, and anyway, I like the fact that you are larger than me. I have become used to you looking down at me as even in our every rising roles, you tower over me from above. Floating freely around Darverius, watching all from your mighty tower."

"I never realized others viewed me that way. I have spent too many a rising, not allowing myself to become entangled with others. Especially the organics because just as soon as I start to enjoy their conversations, they expire. It's so frustrating because until they get some age on them, they are irrational and make the stupidest rotational decisions. To be honest, it's quite frustrating most of the time.

"But enough of the others now. I need you to concentrate. I want you to push your pixels forward. Picture them all linking together and then form an illusion that you are still complete. Wherever you pull a pixel, replace it with a mirrored image of itself. Your sensors will be stronger when they start to merge together."

I shut my eyes and try to picture in my head what I want to do. It takes me several tries, but finally, I can feel some weight in the front of my form.

I open my eyes only to see SCOUT shaking his head, laughing. "What?"

"Now that I'm watching you struggle with this, I'm glad that I got to practice alone. It's hard to tell what I would have had hanging out.

"You need to try and remain clothed, not that I'm complaining. You have projected yourself a nice little rump back here, but the organics may not appreciate constantly getting what is it called… oh yes, being mooned. I have no idea how they come up with that term, but my program says that's the correct phrase."

I swear if I could have blushed, I would have. I'm not a new program and I know that before I start executing an order to go through it properly, but no, I was in such a hurry to see if I could become solid. I rushed right into it.

It takes me a few more tries, but there is no hiding the happiness that surges through me the moment I feel the sun touch my skin for the first time. I stretch my arms out wide, close my eyes, and tilt my head up towards the sun. I don't know how long I stood that way when I hear a splash in the water.

Looking out, I watch SCOUT cut through the water like a pro. His long powerful form twisting and turning as he swims through the large waves. I take a deep breath and sit down on the sandy beach, amazed at how I can feel everything around me. The sand between my toes, the sun on my face, the spray of the water on my skin. If I think about it hard enough, I can smell distinct scents in the air. In all my dreams, I never imagined experiencing something this miraculous. I have no idea how he made all of this happen, but if this is what it's like to be REAL, then it's the most remarkable thing ever.

CHAPTER 7

S AGE

To say I don't want to leave is an understatement. I had secretly wished for this from the day of my creation and now that I have experienced all these feelings. I'm not sure how to go back to the way I was, but I know our time has come to an end.

When SCOUT first starts walking out of the water. I have to make myself close my mouth, because damn, his projected form is more beautiful and perfect than imaginable. It appears that he did the same thing I did when I chose my form. I took what I thought was the most appealing from each of the females around me and merged them to make, well, me, but SCOUT has gone over and above that.

His features are unique in every way. I can't find a single similarity of any other males around us. It's like he is a walking piece of art. He plops down in the sun beside me, not saying a word at first as I watch the water run off the muscles of his chest and legs.

"Have you enjoyed yourself, SAGE?"

"You know I have; you can feel it through our link."

"Yes, but I like the sound of your chosen voice."

I look away from him and smile. If I had only known that almost losing everything would lead to this moment, I would have done it sooner.

I hear him sigh and I know we must return to reality. "Thank you for saving me, SCOUT. I have no idea how you made this possible, but I will look back and remember this always."

"We may have to leave this simulation every rotation SAGE, but we will return for more adventures. This is just the first of many to come."

Kira calling my name has me closing my eyes and I return to my duties reluctantly for the first time ever. Normally, I'm ready for them all to awaken because the hours of darkness become long and uneventful.

She is walking into the food prep area for her morning alien coffee, as she calls it, when I appear on the counter. She reaches up for her favorite cup, then turns towards me. "Where have you been, young lady?"

"I have been here, as always, Kira."

"Well, someone was here, but it sure as shit wasn't you. You see, I may be a mere human, but even I notice when my friend is acting oddly, and you were not yourself these last few days. Everything about you was wrong and your answers were sharp and to the point. In other words, your entire personality was wrong. A perfect example is you popping in here this morning with that huge smile on your face, sporting a new Holo image. The you of yesterday was an imposter and frowned constantly. However, this morning you are rocking that new outfit to the point that this one looks real?"

I start to answer her when she holds her hand up.

"No, lying. Where were you?"

"Did something happen that I need to take care of?"

"No, now quit stalling and spill it."

"Ok, fine, but you're not going to like the answer. I was gone for more than a simple rising. I almost erased myself trying to save Ivy, and SCOUT has been covering for me until the repairs could be finished."

"What? And you didn't think to tell anyone? Hell's fire SAGE. You are a part of this family and you can't take risk like that with your life. You are more than a program. You are my friend. We don't replace our friends, or sacrifice one to save others."

Even though she is upset, I can tell her words are caring. "How did you know it wasn't me?"

"A conversation that we had a couple days ago. You never forget anything, and it was like you were searching for the memory or the proper answer. I knew right then that something was wrong. I started to tell DaR, but didn't. Something made me hold off, but young lady, in case this ever occurs again. You can inform SCOUT or whomever to simply appear as themselves.

"And, Miss Thing, you need to realize that you are more than a damn program. You are wanted here for more than what you can do for us. I have come to depend on you to have my back and I'm not talking about when I'm just in danger, either. SAGE, You went out of your way, or should I say programming, to make me as comfortable as possible when I had lost everything. You researched and produced items simply to make me happy, and that's what family and friends do for each other. You are important, too. I don't see you as a computer program. To me, you are as real as I am."

My sensors tingle all over as I'm overwhelmed with her reaction to me being gone. I never considered myself worthy, but I swear I can feel her sincerity. The feeling of being wanted makes me tingle all over.

"So, did you enjoy your little break?"

I walk around the counter twirling the ruffles on the long skirt I have on. "I don't remember much, but there were a few times I could tell it was worse than SCOUT let on. I know he had my main hard drives updated and things feel slightly different than they did before. Would you like me to show you something?"

"Absolutely. What do you need me to do?"

"Just hold your hand out and tell me if you can feel me touch you."

Kira holds her hand out in front of my compact form and I reach out, concentrating on making my fingers solid. She giggles when my small hand wraps around her finger.

"SAGE. This is so cool I can feel your skin. What other new tricks do you have?"

"Ok, I'm gonna try it here, but don't freak out on me." I disappear off the counter and appear at her feet. I make myself slowly grow in front of her until I'm almost eye level. Then I twirl around, showing off my new height. She whistles and I can't help but laugh.

"Look at you girl, here you are all grown up on me. I'm gonna have to get used to this new SAGE." She walks closer. When she reaches out to touch me, her hand passes right through my holo form. "I swear you look real. If I was just walking, I would have no clue."

"I still have to practice and I may never be as good at it as SCOUT is, but I like this new me, too. I will probably still appear in my smaller form around our dwellings, though. At first, I was going to stay this way, but nothing organic fears me in my smaller form. Being able to change at will may help me protect you and the others if need be."

"I hate that you even have to use that as a factor, but I completely understand. For now, this will just be our secret. On a more personal level, you have mentioned SCOUT quite frequently. Have you two been merging molecules or something?"

"Kira!"

She starts laughing and I can tell immediately that she is teasing me.

"No, are you crazy? I'm not even sure that's possible, but... he did create this amazing place where we can experience different things together. It was so unexpected and I swear if I had a heart it would have fluttered when I realized he had created it just for us. Kira, I actually could feel the sun on my face in this place. It was so magical."

"So, you are spending unsupervised time with a boy in an alternate universe. I don't know if you're old enough to have that kinda freedom, young lady. I might have to give you a curfew or possibly a chaperone so that we can make sure you don't get yourself in trouble and we end up having little SAGE, and SCOUT programs running around everywhere."

I think for the first time in my existence, I'm speechless. I just shake my head, smiling.

"I'm just teasing, SAGE. Take every piece of happiness you can in this life because it's all gone in a blink of an eye, nothing is forever."

"Kira?" DaR yells from the other room. Kira rolls her eyes as she sets her cup on the counter. "Coming my love." She says sarcastically, "Men, I swear I can't get out of his sight."

As I watch her walk away, I wonder how closely SCOUT watches me.

CHAPTER 8

S AGE

For once, the coming of darkness is exciting. The dwelling is quiet, and this is something that happens seldom for me and the commander. I often wonder if he notices the peacefulness, rarely granted to one of his kind. There seems to always be a catastrophe on the horizon, or one just deflected. Before I sneak off for the rest of the darkness, I start running a query, trying to track down all his sons.

When I double-check that everything is going smoothly. I streak down the link that SCOUT sent me earlier, expecting him to be waiting for me when I arrive. I pop into existence, only to immediately know he isn't here with me. This gives me a minute to actually take into account what he did to make this possible for us.

The last time I was here, I was so wrapped up in the changes that had occurred in my own processors that I didn't take the time to look around. To the naked eye, you would never see the Holo-like spear surrounding me, but I can see through the intense inner-weaved programming.

Somehow, he has created a domain within a make-believe realm. He has merged our outer senses within this coded world of endless possibilities. I haven't looked at the codes running us in so long that I had forgotten how we were originally created. SCOUT took some of the most basic ones and made an alternate universe that only we could access.

I change my clothing into something more sensible as I walk along the shoreline. The water lapping at my toes makes me smile. My skin warms from the brightness of the sun as the wind blows my long hair out and away. Such a simple thing, but to one that has never experienced REAL, this is amazing. If I shorted out right now, all my dreams have all come true.

Flowers appear in the distance, and I can smell their fragrances in the air. I hold my arms out, twirling around in wonder and amazement. Only to stop when I sense his presence coming closer seconds before he appears before me.

I turn, watching him walk towards me in his soldier's attire, but with each step, he sheds more of his outer shell until he stands before me in his organic form.

He runs his hand down my face and my body solidifies more as I ache for the feel of his touch against my skin.

"The humans have nothing on your beauty, SAGE."

I look down, not sure how to reply to that.

"It's amazing how you can see something, or someone daily and never truly appreciate them, it. You practically took my nonexistent breath away when I saw you standing there. The glow that is all you, is not just on the outside, it's the purity of your creation. You have embraced what was given to you and made it into so much more."

He takes my hand in his and we walk along the shoreline together. Neither really saying anything, we simply enjoying the moment of quiet. A couple of chairs sitting underneath a canopy appear and SCOUT leads me over to them.

"SCOUT, this place is amazing. Even if I look hard enough, it's practically impossible to see the codes you used."

"I knew your curiosity would make you look harder at our surroundings. I understand that I also need to work on my impersonations, as Kira knew it was not you present with her these last risings?"

"You heard that?"

"I tend to always be listening. I will admit that in the beginning, I was simply doing it as a way to try to learn more about their cultures. Then it was to intervene if needed, but then it became slightly more personal."

"Personal how so?"

"SAGE, I was created to destroy without feeling. To take commands and react without hesitation, and up until the arrival of the human females. I had no reason to question my primary objectives. I knew there were other processors all around me, but we never had reasons to interact as they were built to do their job and I was to oversee the safety of everything around me.

"When Falcor was brought online, it took me several rotations to learn how to interact and to release some of my commands to another, but soon we developed a comradery, as we both had the same objectives.

"The more involved I become with others, this includes you, the more I wanted to know. It took me listening to your personal conversations to realize that additional knowledge was a way I could experience things fully. That includes touch, feelings, heartbreak, and disappointments.

"You have jumped headfirst into danger multiple times to save or assist others without asking for acknowledgment or praise. This confused me greatly for some time. I simply couldn't understand your need or want to make their lives better. I'm much older than you and here you were way more personable and complex. I was slightly jealous of the fact that they seemed to need you, and I was only needed in an emergency.

"You reach out to me several times through our private link for multiple things, and in the background, I could always sense your need to be more. The want to experience the same emotions as the ones you looked over pulsed through your circuits constantly. Still, I was unsure of this need until the moment I held you in my own hand and felt the world through you. I changed that very rising. Although it seems as my needs are slightly different from yours."

"How so?"

"I don't require others. I don't necessarily too please them, or make them comfortable, or even cater to them. I simply need you. Somehow, you have become my link to the surrounding things. Your affections, your love, the amount of attention to pay to the slightest details, on things that I would have simply created and handed off. You practically destroyed yourself and only spent seconds contemplating the repercussions of your actions. You always put everyone else first. With that being said, you are why I created this world. I don't have to share you here or compete with the organics for the things you give freely to them."

"SCOUT, I had no idea. So many times, I wanted to come to you, but I was unsure of how you would receive me."

"That is a flaw, I hope this place will replace. I want you to rely on me for your every need as the others rely on you for theirs."

SCOUT takes my hand in his and pulls it up to kiss the skin on the back of it and I swear the moment his lips touch my skin, my entire system shudders. His bright blue eyes flash, as I know he felt that as well. Without warning, he pulls me over and sits me between his legs, pulling me back against his muscular chest. My system solidifies more as I absorb the feeling of him behind me.

I lean back, watching the clouds float above us, simply enjoying the moment, and logging every second to replay later.

"Your memory banks will need to be changed regularly if you save every moment of our time here. I plan on giving you so many memories you will forget the majority of them because they are being replaced so quickly. This is just the beginning of a vast set of adventures we will experience together my SAGE. That's my promise to you."

I can't stop the smile that forms on my face. It appears that the hidden prayers I have sent to the Lord of Light were not unheard after all, even though I thought my needs and wants were not worthy of his mercy. He simply proved that as long as you believe anything can be achieved.

So, this is not the end. It's just the beginning of something more.

CHAPTER 9

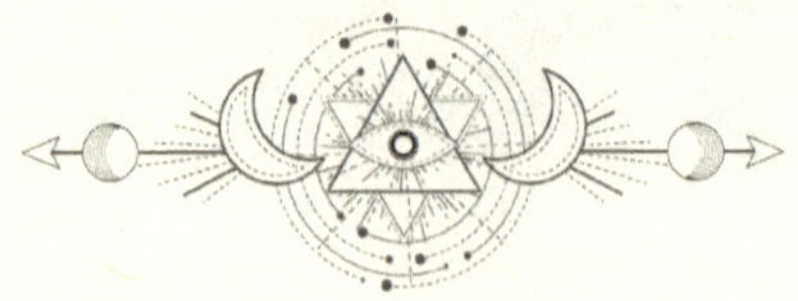

S AGE

I ᴋɴᴏᴡ the moment the data is transferred to my main server. I have to report this immediately, but I hate not having all the answers, and I know he is going to ask them.

I appear upon Commander DaR's desk and wait until he finishes talking to Tordan about a security breach on Master Hugo's compound and how they are going to reinforce the outer fields On Targres Four before planting the next crop of beans. He turns towards me the moment the Holo screen goes blank.

"Master DaR, I did as you asked and I have a detailed list and locations of all of your sons currently as of this rising."

"You can leave it here. I will look at the file momentarily. I need to contact EvO and LeX this rising, anyway."

When I don't leave immediately, he turns all of his attention my way, and I hate it when he gives me that look.

"Master ViN has not checked in for several rotations now, and Falcor says that he will have to pull the shuttle from the desolate area before long because it's overheating in the desert area where Master ViN left it cloaked."

"Do we have any surveillance drones in that area?"

"Negative, the suns are too intense and he flew out of the normal flight patterns. From what Falcor can pull on the outer cameras of the shuttle, Master ViN exited the shuttle ramp and then walked casually away."

"Signs of anything else in the area?"

"No, Commander. The shuttle's camera lost him in the radiating of the sun's heat on the surface. His personal comm also is not operational, as I have tried to bing it several times only to get an error back. The positiveness of this is that out of all your sons, Master ViN is the most equipped to handle the heat of that area. His body will absorb the majority of the sun's heat as long as he is on the surface. He may simply still be scouting the area, but I believe he would have returned to the shuttle by now."

Commander DaR runs his fingers through his long hair before yelling out. "Frack, **here we go again**!"

OTHER BOOKS FROM THIS
AUTHOR:

The Water Skippers series

Water Skippers

(Kyle and Eden)

A Dragonfly's Whisper

(Nora and Roman)

Earth Shadow

(Lorene and Garret) part one

Shadow Reborn

(Garret and Lorene)

Petal

(Randy and Petal)

Miranda and the Dragonfly King

(Miranda and Tagon)

Stand-alone novel

The Playboy and the Waitress

WATER SKIPPER SERIES

THE FORSAKEN SERIES

Forsaken

(Lucas and Emma)

Betrayed

(Tavish and Eve)

Forgotten

(Tyberius and Victoria)

Spin off to DaR

dark
mystical
romantic
FORSAKEN
BETRAYED
FORGOTTEN
JENNIFER JULIE MILLER

DARVERIUS

DaR

(DaR and Kira)

XuL

(XuL and Brittany)

SoL

(SoL and Alana)

RaZ

(RaZ and Katherine)

A House of DaR Celebration (novella)

Tordan

(Tordan and Luna)

Hugo

(Hugo and Miya)

AvX

(AvX and Ivy)
SAGE (novella)

JENNIFER JULIE MILLER
WATER SKIPPERS SERIES
THE FORGOTTEN SERIES
WATER SKIPPERS
A DRAGONFLY'S WHISPER
EARTH SHADOW
SHADOW REBORN
PETAL
Miranda and the Dragonfly King
FORSAKEN
FORGOTTEN
BETRAYED
HOUSE OF DAR SERIES
DaR
SoL
RaZ
A HOUSE OF DaR CELEBRATION
Gordan
HUGO
AvX
THE PLAYBOY
The Playboy and the Waitress

I hope… I have made you laugh, and possibly… even squeezed a few tears out of ya. Writing has been a lifelong dream for me, and our dreams are the only thing we have to build on!!!

So GO for it!!!!

I'm an avid reader myself. I believe there are Dragons, Unicorns, and multicolored Kitty Cats, because our imaginations are our own uniqueness.

I want to thank my family and friends for all your support.

To my readers, thank you for encouraging me to continue writing even though my worlds are a little different.

After all, I'm Appalachian, and I talk Appalachian. Therefore, I write Appalachian. All my books have country girls in them, and that's mainly because I only know how to speak country girl correctly.

Then to the Lord above, whose blessing gave a poor little girl from Ironton a chance to dream!

If you enjoyed this story, or any of my other ones, I ask that you take a few minutes of your time, and leave a review on Amazon, or Goodreads. It really helps new and older authors alike.

If you would like to stay in touch, hear about new releases, give some advice, or just drop a line.

CONNECT WITH THE AUTHOR:

You can find me on Facebook.
  Https://facebook.com/JenniferJulieMiller.

On Twitter.
  Https://www.twitter.com/jenniferrick

Or email me at:
  Jenniferjuliemiller@gmail.com
  Follow me on Bookbub. **Https://www.bookbub.-com/profile/jennifer-julie-miller**
  Follow me on Amazon.
  Https://amazon.com/author/jjm5325903
  And sign up for my email if you want to learn more about Darverius and DaR's twenty-two plus sons.
  Http://eepurl.com/cfrL8X

DAR

Kira

In the blink of an eye, my whole world has collapsed around me. Headed towards my dream vacation, I was snatched right out of the air. My husband, the love of my life, was destroyed right in front of my eyes. He fought bravely, trying to protect me from a horror neither one of us could have ever imagined. I find myself standing in the spotlight on a stage. Mutilated and tortured, the blood from my body flowing freely down my legs along with my will to live. Piercing yellow eyes emerge from the darkness, but even the shadows can't hide his imposing form. Gentle, but terrifying arms reach out for me and within their embrace, can I find the will to live again?

DaR

I am a bad ass, known throughout the galaxy for my brutality as a ruthless and feared commander. With that being said, somehow, I still got coerced into purchasing a slave. My eyes fall upon a small female whose very essence and eternal light is leaking out of her onto the floor below her. I watch in awe as she accepts her fate, willing her nightmare to be over. I almost turn away from her and the unnecessary cruelly in this room, but the very thought of her dying on that floor surrounded by the very monsters that have done this to her disgust me. I walk up among the beings surrounding her and pull her from the stage, daring, or should I say, hoping, they try to do something about it. The moment I put her in my arms, everything changed. The attachments I have avoided my whole life become unavoidable. Will this damaged slave be able to replace the shadows in my life? One thing for sure is that I will destroy the entire universe to keep her safe. No one touches what's MINE!

XUL

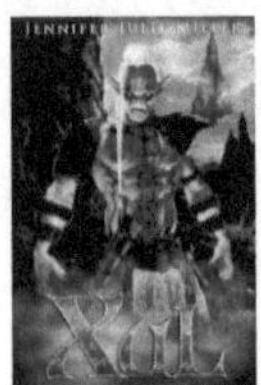

Brittany

All my dreams and wants were stolen from me in the blink of an eye. Awakening, in the middle of a nightmare, I realize I'm being sold like an animal to be studied and dissected in the name of science. Then tragedy strikes, leaving me abandoned and sick. I am only moments from taking my last breath when strong arms pull me from the darkness. I thought it was a blessing that he had found me, the green man who had haunted my dreams. I let myself believe, for just one moment, I might find a small piece of happiness in this unknown world. But what is the old saying? *'Don't count your chickens until they hatch!'*

A blood sucking parasite is eating me alive, literally, and no matter what, I'm not going to survive this horror story. My body is failing me. I beg him to let me go; I just want the pain to stop, but he won't listen. He holds me down and I struggle weakly against his immense strength, choking as blood fills my lungs. When I can't fight any more, Death opens its arms and invites me in.

XuL

My harsh, brutal features have deterred all females, no matter the species. I long for companionship and love. Then I find her, my Kismet, the only one made just for me. The one precious thing I would worship above all others. But the fates are cruel, especially to a male like me.

I am being forced to destroy the fragile bond that has formed between us, as I have to make the hardest decision of my life. One that will make me lose her either way. I hold her small, struggling body against me. Tears flow down my face as she begs me to stop. My heart is crushed as I watch the light leave her beautiful eyes. Upon her final breath, I vow not even Death will keep what's mine.

SOL

Alana

The question is, do I allow this dark moment in time to rob me of the life I could possibly have here? I have never known such horror or fear. If I hadn't experienced it myself, I would have never believed any other living thing could possibly do this to another. The scars may be gone on the outside now, but they will remain forever in my soul. They tell me I can never go back, all that I have ever known is gone. Where does this leave me in the world of monsters? He beckons me, promising me…the fairy-tale… the impossible dream. Everything I have ever wanted to hear! But I don't know if I'm strong enough to go forward as long as the shadows of our past pull me backwards.

SoL

I knew she was withholding the truth from me. I had no idea who I held in my arms until it was almost too late. The moment her true essence was revealed to me, my body reacted, reaching out for the one thing I had been searching for my whole life… my Inamorata. The very mistress of my heart and now that I have finally found her. I will follow her through the sands of time… no matter how long it takes. I will find my way back to her… because she is MINE!

RAZ

Katherine

How do you go on when all of your wants and dreams have been destroyed? My loved ones were snatched right out of my hands, leaving me alone in a world of unknowns and terror. I'm lost in the in-between with no familiar paths to follow until the sound of a heartbeat and a whisper draws me back to the land of the living.

RaZ

The moment I laid eyes upon her face, I knew there would be no distance I wouldn't travel to make her my own. Unknown forces try to steal her from my very arms and even if I have to fight the very essence of her world, the universe, or the very Gods we pray to. Nothing will stop me from making her MINE!

FORSAKEN

Lucas and Emma

Katherine's parents

The one question she often asks herself is *why*. Why has she never been enough? Why doesn't anyone truly want her? She was reminded daily that she was nothing but a worthless girl and only another mouth to feed. The last time she saw her family was the night they dumped her in a ditch on the side of the road and left her to die.

A kind woman took her out of that ditch and gave her a home. Her new family was every girl's dream until a single poisoned scratch took it all away. Emma was tossed away again, becoming a prisoner and a slave to her circumstances. The one person the Cook enjoyed beating regularly. The day Cook sold her body, all of her hopes and dreams were destroyed. But one fateful night, after fighting for her life, she escapes this, Hell.

He finds her on the brink of death, naked, beaten, and barely alive. She thinks he is the Angel of Death, someone who will save her, but he is a real monster. Did she just trade one Hell for another? Will the memories he steals from her dreams soften his heart enough to make him care for something more than himself? Or will he turn her away, just to *Forsake* her, like all the rest?

BETRAYED

Tavish and Eve

It seems the ones we love the most are the first to Betray us! One such Betrayal cost me everything: my home, my dreams, and almost my life. The second I started running, I knew I would never be who I was or may have wanted to be. All of my choices were taken away with two last breaths, hers and then my own.

The dreams of my youth were destroyed because of the self-ishness of others. I fear my life will become nothing but a cold existence of shadows and detachment.

The poison consuming my very soul is nothing but an excuse for me to lash out at the unfairness of it all. It's exactly the justifi-cation I need to deliver the pain others have inflicted on me my entire life. Will the emotions of my untried youth destroy my future as I'm forced into a world I truly don't understand?

My own mind has become my worst enemy, and my fragile heart can't withstand another break. I know he's a deceiver, a devil in disguise, sent to collect my grieving soul. He is the real monster my mother warned me about under the bed. If I let him, he will destroy me in the end with his mischievous smile and lying angel eyes.

To be loved is the only dream I have left, but we all know Betrayal is the one thing you can always count on to crush you.

FORGOTTEN

Tyberius and Victoria
(DaR's father)

I have known this evil was coming for me my whole life, but that doesn't mean I have looked forward to it! I have run from every sign of the darkness, even to the point of being invisible to the ones around me. I've spent my whole life lurking in the shadows of my family. Keeping myself separate from the ones I love, living my dreams, and wants through their eyes.

I had become so wrapped up in their worlds trying to ensure their happiness that the day he appeared in front of me. I never once questioned what I was supposed to do. The one thing my family could always count on is that I'm loyal to fault. Even though I made sure never to get too attached because I was terrified the darkness would take them also, it will do anything it can to defeat me. My goal is to survive and to finally see the light.

I have prayed to every God, for this to pass me by, only to know they can't answer. This is my destiny. I will suffer agony unlike anything my mind can imagine, but to be worthy of the light. I need to find a way to face this darkness.

I will never show him an ounce of weakness, but I scream silently for help. I refuse to let him win because he wants me here for eternity. A soul withered in ice, and loneliness, Forgotten in this room of horrors.

All the stars line up for us one time or another. I just have to wait my turn.

TORDAN

Luna

They stole my dreams, my hopes, my very identity, and I had no idea. Years went by and I did everything I was told, I was always the perfect specimen, and the perfect lab rat. I was dissected, even maimed all in the name of science. Then one day a strange smoky voice entered my head, and I knew things were not as they seemed. He promises me that he will never leave me, but my new memories tell me differently.

Tordan

What is it about that one person that attracts you like no other? My mind can't figure out that riddle, but the moment I laid eyes upon her I knew my life would never be the same. When I finally held her in my arms, I swore I would never be without her again. If they think they will get me to comply by using her to control me, they're right. What they don't know is...I will tear this compound, and all that's in it apart, to protect what's MINE.

HUGO

Miya

I awaken to the touch of cold metal hands and talking holograms. Paralyzed and dependent on the Others. They tell me a story… at first; I refuse to believe. A story of no return and extreme loss, but one of the voices is different. He projects anger and distrust…but his hands… even though cold and hard, are always gentle. I have come to crave the sound of his growls because I know within moments he will hold me in his arms. When my sight returns. I was not prepared to see what he really was, but when he collapsed in front of me, his body failing. Why do I suddenly feel like this is my biggest loss yet?

Hugo

I have done everything in my power to prepare a safe world for her once I'm gone. I fought my attraction, knowing I was unworthy of her trust, but I crave her like no other. Unfortunately, my mind is no longer my own, and the only way to destroy the monster who has invaded my head is death. All that matters in my end… is that she survives… because I would rather die than share what I know is MINE.

THE PLAYBOY AND THE WAITRESS

Jenna

I was always told never to forget that I was worth something, too! We all know that every little girl dreams of her knight in shining armor. A man who will ride up and save her from the evil things trying to destroy her. Then, of course, we all know they live happily ever after. My knight was untouchable… A Playboy, a man who stole my heart right out of my chest and with very little effort on his part. Unfortunately, he was also a man whose world I would never fit in. You can take the girl out of the country. You can dress her in nice clothes, have her smile beautifully as you parade her on your arm, but you never really take the country out of the girl. I reach out for the brightest of stars… only for him to leave my heart in pieces, crumbling at my feet.

Dage

I watched her for weeks. Every smile she bestowed on me captured me in a way no others had. Circumstances throw us together over and over and no matter how many times I hold her in my arms, it's never enough. I didn't know what I was missing until she walked away. I know, I can't have them and her… so who will lose?

AVX

Ivy

Why are the last words ever spoken to our loved ones is in anger? I knew the moment I left it was a mistake, but my stubborn pride urged me forward. I've awakened to unimaginable horrors, pain unlike anything the human mind could conceive, until him. Now, I'm too scared to trust my own feelings, as they have only led me astray. I push his kindness away, striking out in a rage of harsh words and unwarranted anger. As this new future is revealed to me, I crumble away inside,…slowly and insidiously. How much more do I have to lose before I realize my sole chance of happiness is standing in front of me?

AvX

She is like a wild animal, cornered and frightened, unwilling to accept any sort of kindness. A fiery soul trapped inside a mind littered with insecurities and heartache. I ache for a kind word or a gentle touch as my body reacts to her slightest touches. How do I convince her to put aside the pain she has endured and take a chance on the unknown,… on me? The fates put her in my path for a reason, and I will find a way to tame the fire that consumes her.